L-19/p-0.5

Yellow Umbrella Books are published by Capstone Press
151 Good Counsel Drive, P.O. Box 669, Mankato, Minnesota 56002
http://www.capstone-press.com

Library of Congress Cataloging-in-Publication Data
Weidenman, Lauren.
    What is a map?/by Lauren Weidenman.
    p. cm.
    Includes index.
    ISBN 0-7368-0742-X
    1. Maps—Juvenile literature. [1. Maps.] I. Title.
GA105.6. W43   2001
910—dc21
                                                        00-036670

        Summary: Describes various types of maps, as well as compass roses, and map keys.

Editorial Credits:
Susan Evento, Managing Editor/Product Development; Elizabeth Jaffe, Senior Editor;
    Sydney Wright and Charles Hunt, Designers; Kimberly Danger and Heidi Schoof,
    Photo Researchers

Photo Credits:
Cover: Barbara Comnes; Title Page: Index Stock Imagery (top), Index Stock Imagery and/Eric
Oxendorf (bottom); Page 2: Greg Vaughn/TOM STACK & ASSOCIATES; Page 4: Index Stock
Imagery and/Tony Casper/Picture Cube; Page 6: Index Stock Imagery; Page 10-11: Index Stock
Imagery; Page 12: Index Stock Imagery and/Eric Oxendorf; Page 14: Don Hamerman/New
England Stock Photo (left), New England Stock Photo/Jean Higgins (right); Page 15: Jim
Pickerell (left), Shaffer Photography/James L. Shaffer (right); Page 16: Shaffer
Photography/James L. Shaffer

Art on pages 3, 5, 7, 8, 9, 10 (inset), and 13 by Kathleen Kuchera

2 3 4 5 6 06 05 04 03 02

WHAT IS A MAP?

By Lauren Weidenman

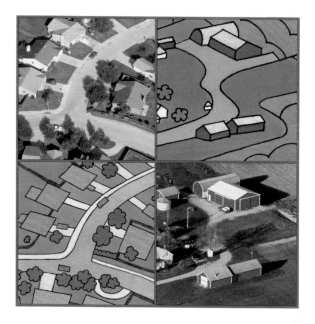

Consulting Editor: Gail Saunders-Smith, Ph.D.
Consultants: Claudine Jellison and
Patricia Williams, Reading Recovery Teachers
Content Consultant: Andrew Gyory, Ph.D., American History

Yellow Umbrella Books

an imprint of Capstone Press
Mankato, Minnesota

What is a map?
A map is a drawing
that shows what a place
looks like from above.

This picture shows what a beach
looks like from above.

This is a map of that beach.
Find the sand, the water,
and the trees on this map.
What else can you find
on this map?

Here is a picture of a garden.

Maps use colors to show things.
This map shows the flowers
in the garden.

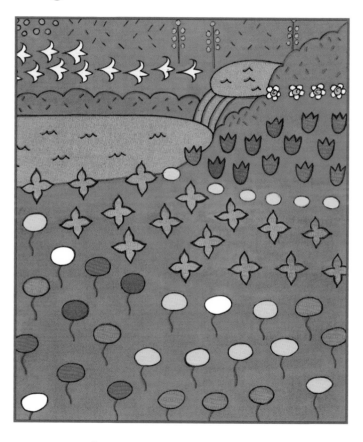

Can you find the purple flowers
on this map?

This picture shows
what a neighborhood
looks like from above.

This is a map of that
neighborhood. What can you
see from above that you
cannot see from the ground?

A map can show a small place.
A bedroom is a small place.

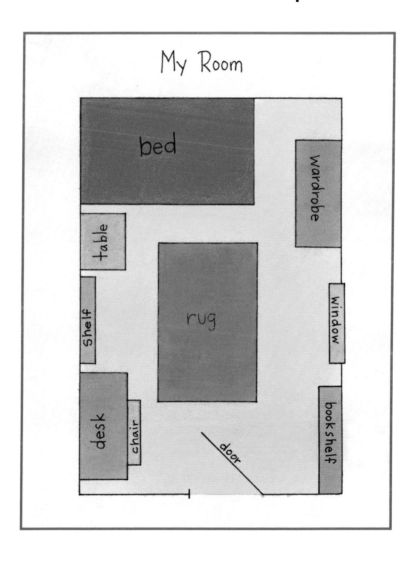

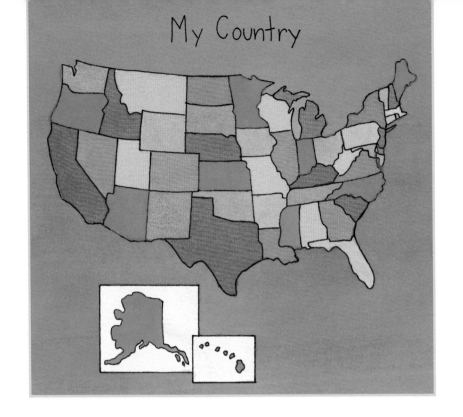

A map can show a big place.
This map shows the United States.
The United States is much bigger
than a bedroom.
But the maps are
about the same size.

The compass rose on a map
helps you read direction.

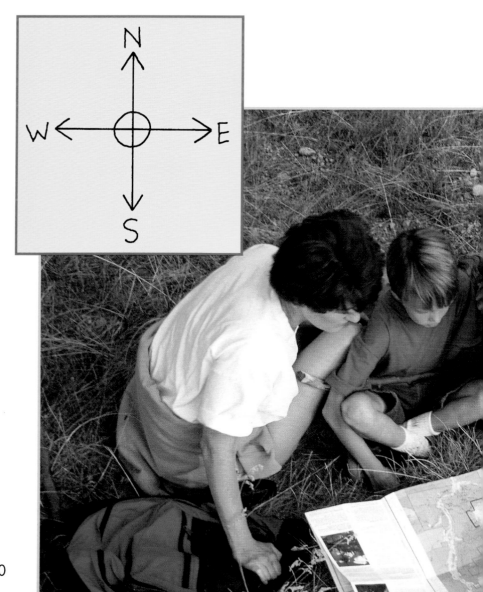

North is at the top of a map.
South is at the bottom.
East is on the right, and
west is on the left.

Symbols are pictures
that stand for something.
Symbols help you read maps too.

21024

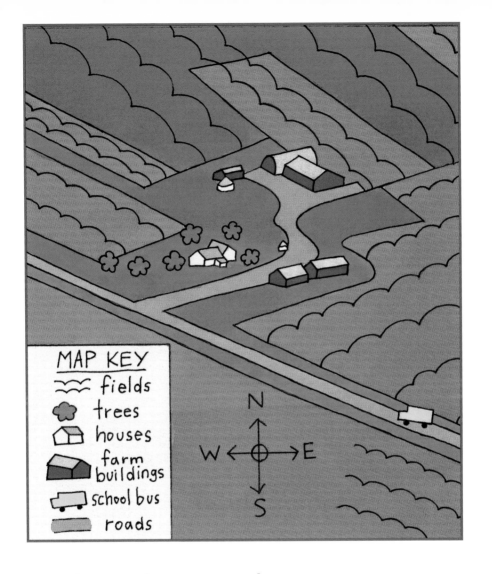

Look at the map key.
It shows what the symbols
on this map mean.

People use maps
in many ways.
They use maps
to help find
where things are.

They use maps
to get from
place to place.

People use maps to find places in their state.

They also use maps to find places in their country.

When can you use maps?

Words to Know/Index

Word Count: 266
Early-Intervention Level: 14